Making Friends

Katya from Moscow and Star from
San Francisco: two eleven-year-old girls
discover America together

Photography by
Morton Beebe

 Henry Holt and Company New York　　 **Raduga Publishers Moscow**

Credits:
U.S. Coordinator: Patricia Montandon
U.S.S.R. Coordinator: Alevtina Fedulova
Photography: Morton Beebe
Designer: James Stockton
Editor: Peder Jones
Translator: Dimitri Agrachev

It is with great pleasure that we acknowledge the
following people who worked in the spirit of
peaceful cooperation to create this book: Soviet
Consul General Valentin Kamenev, Barbara Ross,
Virginia Garrison, John Pritzker, Fred Hill, Fran
G. Birks (*photo page 28*), Mark Pokempner, Click/
Chicago (*photo page 29*), Darryl Hartley-Leonard,
Novosti Press (*photo pages 94–95*).

Raduga Publishers would also like to thank the
Soviet Peace Committee and the Soviet Peace
Fund for their great help in getting this book
together. Indeed, it would never have been possible
without them.

Published in the United States by
Henry Holt and Company, Inc., 521 Fifth Avenue,
New York, New York 10175.

Published in Canada by Fitzhenry & Whiteside Limited,
195 Allstate Parkway, Markham, Ontario L3R 4T8.

Library of Congress Catalog Card Number: 87-45356

ISBN: 0-8050-0641-9

First American Edition

Published simultaneously in the U.S.S.R. by Raduga Publishing
Company, Moscow.

Composition by American Typesetting, Inc., Los Angeles.

Printed in the U.S.S.R. by Production Amalgamation
"Ivan Fiodorov Printing House," Leningrad.

10 9 8 7 6 5 4 3 2 1

ISBN 0-8050-0641-9

Dedicated to: The children of the world who want to grow up in peace and the children who are at this moment besieged, orphaned and homeless because of a war in their country.

This isn't play:
The weapons are real.
And the children cry out,
in agony, anger, surprised
that adults would deny
their future,
their dreams,
their lives.
For what? a piece of land?
a medal? power?
Soft wailing noises;
and then
a giant nuclear shadow
is pushed back by
light-filled hands
of the Children
who want to live,
who want to love . . .
to have children of their own.

Dream freely of the future—I think only children can do that. When you are young, you have the special privilege of imagining yourself becoming the world's most famous scientist or movie star or writer, or even all three at once.

A future of almost magical possibilities is what all children should be able to see. But today many of our young people see no future at all for themselves. The threat of nuclear war blackens their dreams. My own son Sean made me aware of just how deeply children fear nuclear annihilation—and of how the feeling of helplessness, of not being able to do anything to prevent an approaching disaster, makes the fear all the worse.

It was in response to my son's feelings that I founded Children as the Peacemakers in 1982. I hoped that this organization would give children opportunities to express their concerns about war, and work constructively together with adults for world peace. We have organized international peace trips every year since 1982, and have had so many gratifying experiences. On these trips children of ages eight to fourteen have traveled to China, Eastern Europe, the Middle East, and many other regions, and have talked with such leaders as Chancellor Helmut Kohl of West Germany and the late Indira Gandhi of India about the need for friendship among all nations.

In 1985 Children as the Peacemakers invited children from thirty-three nations to San Francisco to be honored for works of peace. We also invited Jane Smith, mother of Samantha Smith, to join us and accept an award honoring her late daughter. The memories of Samantha and her efforts for world peace were so overwhelming then, though, that I couldn't help but feel that something more should be done.

An idea came to me in the middle of a daydream—"Why not invite a Soviet girl to come on a peace trip to America, a trip just like the one Samantha took to the USSR?" Jane Smith shared my enthusiasm for the idea, and so did the Soviet Peace Committee. They and many other people worked long hours to put together a whirlwind trip of epic proportions. We decided together that on her friendship trip the Soviet girl should have an American friend with whom she could share her experiences, and perhaps even welcome to the USSR on a similar visit someday.

We soon learned that our visitor would be an eleven-year-old named Katerina Lycheva. We learned a little about her background: Her home was in Moscow, her mother was a scientific research worker and her father was a commercial advertising specialist; she was attending an English-language school, she had musical talent, and she loved dogs. But those were facts on paper. What would the real Katya be like, we wondered. We also wondered how she would take to her American traveling partner, Star Rowe.

I already knew Star to be an exceptional young person. The daughter of a San Francisco street artist, she was at age ten a remarkably skillful ballet dancer. Star had won the honor of accompanying Katya by writing an essay on peace and creating an original ballet entitled "A Prayer of Peace."

So I was naturally quite excited as I flew east to meet little Katya and welcome her to our country. But I felt anxious, too, wondering how it would all work out. Would the children be able to stand the rigors of such a fast-paced trip? Would they get along with each other? Would the people of America be interested in Katya and Star and their message? And what of the future? Could this be the beginning of an exchange program between the USA and the USSR?

I need not have worried. Katya and Star both were absolutely wonderful, and they were received warmly everywhere we went. Not only that, they truly became friends, showing the truth of what Samantha said after her visit with Soviet children: "It seemed strange to even talk of war when we got along so well together. . . . If we could be friends by just getting to know each other better, then what are our two countries really arguing about?"

Wonderful things have continued to happen since the historic trip. Star and I have been to the USSR, where she was able to renew her friendship with Katya, and they had the chance to talk about world peace with the President of the USSR, Andrei Gromyko. Children as the Peacemakers has also completed another peace mission, this time taking children from eight nations on a peace tour of Norway, the Soviet Union, India, Hong Kong, China, and Japan.

Our concern for a safe planet embraces all the children everywhere.

Yet at the end of each trip, along with the joy there comes a feeling of sadness and a sense of renewed concern. The journey has been completed, but the destination has not been reached . . . the goal of world peace remains distant. We realize now that it will take more than these few visits to ensure that the children's message of peace is truly heard; and so we and our friends in the Soviet Union have dedicated ourselves to the task of establishing a regular peace exchange program, through which exemplary young people of our two nations can further the dialogue of peace and mutual understanding.

Making Friends, is part of this effort to give the children of the world hope for their future. Though it is about two special girls, it also tells the story of young people everywhere who share the dream of a world free from war and its devastation. This book belongs to you, too, because you can help us work toward the safe and beautiful future of which we all dream.

In Peace and Love,

Patricia Montandon

The world is a small planet; its children are its future. As adults our responsibility is to guarantee our children's future—to provide a basis for hope, to ensure that political, economic, or social differences do not compromise their future or ours.

We live in a unique time in the evolution of humankind: the nuclear age. In the past forty years many secrets of the atom have been unraveled. This has given us access to almost unlimited sources of energy. But like all technologies, nuclear energy is a Pandora's box with almost unlimited potential for good *or* evil. If properly used, now or in the future, nuclear energy can benefit humankind. For example, physicians use radiation to lessen the effects of cancer. Yet, as we know too well, nuclear energy is also used to produce military weapons. In this form—if employed—it can destroy our civilization. Fear of nuclear war haunts each of us. It is not uncommon for young children, when asked, to indicate their greatest fear by speaking not of dragons or other mythical beasts, but of the threat of nuclear war.

I am pleased to introduce this book because I believe there is much we can learn from children. *Making Friends* is the story of two girls: one Soviet, the other American. But in a real sense it is about *all* children. It is a book written by children. A book written for children. But I believe it is also written for adults.

The relationship between the United States and the Soviet Union is not child's play. Most adults are distressed to encounter things that are different, new things, be they individuals, societies, or political systems. Our reaction to the unfamiliar is often to discriminate, to limit, to define, even to restrict dialogue—all because of fear. If one needs a pointed example of this it is worth reading Jerzy Kosinski's *The Painted Bird*. But is this fearful response sensible or even possible in an age of nuclear weapons?

Children's reactions to the new, the different, are unlike those of most adults. Theirs are usually reactions of curiosity, of interest—not of fear. Imagine the surprise and delight of a young Soviet girl such as Katya on seeing the Statue of Liberty for the first time, or of Star's first encounter with Moscow's St. Basil's Cathedral. Their feelings are similar: surprise, delight, curiosity. Communication and understanding follow that immediately transcend geographic and cultural boundaries.

In an age when our technologies can either advance humankind or end civilization, each of us must do all we can to listen to our children, to be certain our technologies are used for peaceful purposes. Perhaps in this mission we can take a lesson from their enthusiasm, curiosity, and optimism, their inherent trust of others—in short, their belief in the future.

—Robert Peter Gale, M.D.

Dr. Gale, the American doctor who risked his life for the victims of the Chernobyl nuclear accident, is the father of three children, aged three, eight, and ten.

Chicago

Katya: When I left Moscow to fly to the United States, I was really thrilled. To take a peace trip in memory of Samantha Smith was like a dream come true for me. My mummy Marina Ignatieva, Alevtina Fedulova, who works for the Soviet Peace Committee, and Dimitri Agrachev, our interpreter, were my companions from home. I was excited as I had never traveled away from the Soviet Union before.

We flew first to Montreal, Canada, a trip of twelve hours. We were met there by Patricia Montandon, the lady who sponsored the trip for "Children as the Peacemakers." When I first saw her at the airport, tall with a lovely and kind face, I thought, "She looks like the fairy godmother from 'Cinderella.'" She was dressed in a light-colored suit, with a long flowing cape that reached almost all the way down to the floor. She welcomed us and flew with us to Chicago—our first stop in the U.S.A.

A fair-haired girl about my age with a huge bunch of white roses was waiting for us at the Chicago airport. That was Star Rowe. Patricia had already told me that Star had been in a contest for the right to be my traveling companion. She had written an essay about peace and composed a dance called "Peace Prayer," and had won the contest.

Star gave me the roses and we embraced. She welcomed me in Russian, and I greeted her in English. We became friends at once.

Star: I was excited when I learned my essay on peace had won a trip for me to accompany Katerina Lycheva during her five-city tour of the United States. I had never been to any of the cities we were going to, so it was all the more interesting for me. But I was *really* excited when I went to the Chicago airport to greet Katya. I pictured her to have short, black, curly hair and to be skinny, but I was wrong. She did have short hair, but she didn't have curly black hair. She had straight blonde hair and a great big smile, and beautiful green eyes.

When I saw all the press people, I got very nervous, but I tried not to shake. I had brought white roses and baby's-breath for Katya and her friends. When she got out of the plane and I saw her, I suddenly noticed all the flashing lights of the photographers, but I didn't let them bother me. Katya was wearing a knitted cap and ski pants and colored socks. I gave her the flowers and said my speech in Russian. I wasn't nervous anymore. And then we stood and giggled together about all the questions the press were asking. But as we left the airport, Pat had to call a doctor because Katya was sick; she had a very bad cold. Even so, she still smiled for all the people who came to see her.

Star nervously awaited Katya's arrival, holding a welcoming bouquet. Neither she nor anyone else had expected such an overwhelming turnout by the press.

At last Katya arrived, carrying the Children as the Peacemakers flag . . . and wearing a great big smile. She was with her mom, Marina, an interpreter named Dimitri, and Alevtina Fedulova, who is the executive secretary of the Soviet Peace Committee. Patricia had a hard time learning to pronounce Alevtina's name.

The next day we went to a "Welcome to the United States, Katya" breakfast, where we got to cook in the Hyatt Hotel kitchen. We cooked scrambled eggs. Imagine me, cooking my own breakfast in a hotel! Then we went to where they make cookies and cakes. There were kids from a school and so many members of the press that I couldn't eat. After that, we went to the La Salle Language Academy and did sixth grade work. We did geometry in one class, and we talked about peace in another. We also exchanged gifts with the kids. It was nice finding out how other children felt about peace. I felt good knowing that I had new friends. Katya was still sick, but we were the only ones who knew it.

The Hyatt Hotel had a "Welcome to the United States" breakfast for Katya. She and Star got to wear chef's caps and cook. The hotel even had a message for Katya in Russian. Everyone was happy to meet the "little ambassador from Russia."

Katya: In math period at the La Salle Academy we were asked to sit in front. The teacher gave us square boards with little nails sticking out, and we were told to put rubber bands on the nails to make different shapes—triangles, squares, and so on. It was fun.

When the teacher asked us to make an octagon, Star began to look around for help. She didn't know what an octagon looks like. It was the first time I ever heard that word. The girls who sat next to us began whispering and tried to show us what to do. We were very glad they did that because we didn't want to look silly. And I thought, "American kids whisper just like us. We're no different when it comes to prompting friends."

One of the kids was making too much noise and the teacher told him to stop it. For a moment I quite forgot that I was in an American school and not in my own. Everything looked so familiar. The teacher was just as strict, but—even more important—learning was just as much fun. I wanted to stay until the end of the lesson, but the teacher told us that we had to leave because the other kids at the school were anxious to see us. I wanted to see them, too.

I saw a piano near the door, and I decided to play and sing our Russian song "Katyusha" for the kids there. But the piano lid would not open, and the teacher and I started to pull at it in different

It was an all-American day for Katya. She and Star went to the La Salle Language Academy in Chicago and were taught how to make different shapes with rubber bands on a nail board. The classrooms were off limits to the press except for five minutes.

ways. It was supposed to slide in and not pop up the way I'm used to. We just stood there, each pulling our own way, and then we laughed when we realized what was happening. So I sang, and Star sang "La-la-la," because of course she did not know the words. She and the other kids told me they liked the song very much.

Star: We had a good lunch—hot dogs, ice cream and milk—at the La Salle Language Academy, and they had Soviet and American flags on the table. Then we sang "We Are the World," and that was fun, too. When we left the school, we went to a peace museum and saw beautiful pictures, paintings, and lots of peace ribbons. Katya and I were given several books about peace.

Katya: In the peace museum I learned a lot about women who work against nuclear war. These women set up tents outside a big nuclear weapons base and live in them. They tell everyone that they want the base shut down for good. I remember their slogan: "Men used to go to war, now women go for peace!"

The people at the museum gave me an interesting game. It's called "Peace by Peace." You have to make a city of the future out of a thousand pieces. And it's a city of peace.

(left) Katya brought paper "peace doves," which she gave out to the schoolchildren. They filled in their names and addresses so they each could become pen pals with a Soviet child.
(below) The girls admired the paintings in the peace museum.

Katya: We went straight from the museum to see Harold Washington, the mayor of Chicago. In Moscow I had heard on TV that Harold Washington had declared his city nuclear-free. I liked the mayor at once.

Star: Mayor Washington gave Katya and me each a teddy bear that had a shirt that read Chicago Bears, and he made a proclamation saying it was Children as the Peacemakers Day—and Katya Lycheva Day—in Chicago.

Katya: As soon as we left the mayor's office, Star and I began to play with the bears the mayor had given us. I called mine Winnie, and Star called hers Brownie. Our bears played and talked and even danced with each other all the way to the hotel.

Star: We were glad when we finally got to go back to the Hyatt Hotel to rest. Katya was feeling better but had jet lag. We were all very tired.

Mayor Harold Washington of Chicago gave the group a grand welcome. Katya and Star hugged their Chicago bears, which is also the name of Chicago's famous football team.

Katya: The next day we were invited to the Children's Museum. I was surprised to see that what was called a museum was really something like our Pioneers' Palace. It was a kind of many-colored fair with booths and stands where kids could try different professions.

We had a great guide. His name was Joshua, he was thirteen, and he said he spent a lot of his time at the museum. Joshua took us to a stand where some kids were learning to play computer

games. Joshua did very well, but Star and I lost at our games. In another booth, however, the people told us we were rather promising interior decorators. We also spent some time trying to learn the art of flower arrangement. Then we met some girls who were learning ballet, and Star and I tried to stand on the tips of our toes. I saw a young man sitting in the middle of the room signing autographs for the kids. Joshua explained that he was a movie star. I tried to imagine one of our famous actors sitting in the Pioneers' Palace signing his pictures. That would be funny, because it would be so unusual. But I like the idea.

The young movie actor gave me his autograph. I gave him my own signed picture in return, because I have been in the movies, too.

I remember especially talking to young women from Greenpeace. They explained that their organization was for peace and was also trying to protect all living things. At their invitation I planted a chamomile seed in a tub filled with earth. Then I told them about the Peace Gardens that kids in my country planted in memory of the Soviet people who died in the war against fascism, so that we kids would be able to live on this planet. It had been the kids' own idea, and they wrote about it in a children's magazine called *Pioneer.* Now there are gardens like that all over the Soviet Union. I thought it would be a good idea if American kids joined us in this, so I wrote a letter to all American kids and gave it to the editor of *National Geographic World.* In the letter I suggested that we plant trees and flowers together and make one big Peace Garden for all children.

Star: That night we went to a family's home for dinner. The Chicago International Center had arranged that Katya and the people traveling with her would be able to visit an American family. At dinner I accidently squirted whipped cream on the girl that was across the table, and everyone laughed. After laughing together about the flying whipped cream, Katya and I became closer.

(above left) Ronald McDonald led Katya into a McDonald's restaurant for a typical American hamburger and fries. "I liked Ronald McDonald very much, but not so very much the hamburger," Katya said, and then added, "the fries, well, they were delicious."

(right) At the Children's Museum, the girls were shown different shapes and were able to play with colors and paints. But Katya enjoyed planting a chamomile seed for peace the best of all.

Katya: In the evening we went to visit a family called the Maces. Two girls about my age were there, as well as a fifteen-year-old boy. Star and I were impatient to get there, and we asked the driver again and again how far it was. The driver got tired of our questions and said, "When you see a crowd of press people, you'll know we are there." He was quite right. When we got out of the car, a big crowd

(right) The girls were fascinated by the computer that was displayed at the Children's Museum. Katya used it to send a message to the world: "Mir," which means "peace" in Russian. (below) Katya and Star learn about flower arranging.

The girls exchanged gifts with members of the Mace family.

was waiting: our hosts, kids, a lot of neighbors and the press. There were other people, too, who had come a long way because they had read in the newspapers that the Mace family was going to host a Soviet girl and they wanted to give gifts and letters. I was very touched.

There was a big poster on the front of the house that said, "Здравствовайте, Катерина!", which means "Welcome, Katerina!", only nobody at home calls me Katerina, and the Russian word for *welcome* was spelled all wrong. I couldn't help smiling, but I had a very nice warm feeling because our hosts had found somebody who had written those two words in Russian as best he could.

Star and I quickly got to know Christie, her friend Julie, and her brother Mike. When we sat down to dinner, our hosts began talking very fast, and I could

not follow what they said. I became bored, but Star helped me out. Quite by chance she pushed her napkin next to my plate. I pushed it back to her. Then we began running around the table, throwing the napkin back and forth, until Mummy took it away from us.

After that game ended, we went to Christie and Mike's room and began to play tag. It was not a very large room, but that only made the game more fun. When we crash-landed on the beds, we tried not to do it too hard, so I don't think the mess we made was too terrible. Next Mike took out his toy musical instruments and we formed a band. Christie played a pipe, I was at the piano, and Star danced. Mike was the conductor at first, but then he saw what an excellent band we were and ran to get his camera and took pictures.

When Christie introduced me to her dog, I confessed to her that I love animals more than anything and told her I'd even made a wish on New Year's Day that I would get a puppy.

The time passed very quickly. We were playing hide-and-seek when Mummy called that it was time to say goodbye. We didn't want to go yet, so we decided that the grown-ups were going to be "it" for our last game. Only we didn't tell them about it—we just hid all over the place, so they were quite surprised when they didn't find us in any of the rooms. Our mothers were beginning to worry when we leapt out of our hiding places.

We kids still didn't want to leave, and the adults were rather sad, too. I could see they had become friends with the Maces and their guests like we had with Christie, Mike, and Julie. I gave everyone picture postcards of Moscow and put a Soviet Peace Committee scarf over our hostess's head.

The whole family went out on the lawn to see us off, and it was clear that they were sad to see us go. Star and I wanted very much to stay and play with the kids some more.

In the morning we flew to New York. I had already taught Star some Russian. She proved to be a very good student. She could say a few phrases without any accent. The phrase she liked best was "Ты устала?", which means "Are you tired?" She asked me that every five minutes. At first I replied graciously, "No, I'm not," every time, but after a while I begged her, "please, Star, let's try some other question." Then she learned how to ask, "Do you like to watch TV?" On all the following days I kept telling her, "No, I'm not tired and yes, I like to watch TV."

Katya and Star had a fine time learning about personal computers.

New York

Star: When Katya and I first got to New York, we looked at all the press and were amazed. There were at least one hundred people, all waiting to talk with us! We had a press conference, and lights were flashing all the time. I could hardly see. Katya and I talked about America and Russia and New York and how much alike we all are. The adults didn't say anything to us, but I overheard that there had been a death threat to Katya. Suddenly we had lots of police and men with earphones guarding us. It was scary. I wondered if Katya knew. I also wondered why anyone would want to hurt Katya.

The next day we went to the "Today" show, and Katya, Pat, and Dimitri (the interpreter) were interviewed by Jane Pauley. While they were being interviewed, I was in the NBC Green Room watching the "Today" show on television. Tony Bennett was there, and I met a man who was one hundred years old. It was his birthday.

Sightseeing in New York included a visit to the top of the Empire State Building. Here Katya's mother snaps a picture of her daughter on top of the world.

Katya: I was thrilled to meet Samantha Smith's mother when we came to the television interview at CBS. I was sorry that the meeting was very short and that nobody had told us in advance. All I had with me were a few Soviet postage stamps with pictures of Samantha, and a song about her, performed by the Moscow Children's Choir, called "Red Carnation." I gave the stamps and the song to Jane Smith and told her that I had also brought a great pile of back issues of the newspaper *Pionerskaya Pravda* and of *Pioneer* magazine with articles about her daughter, as well as a lot of letters from Soviet children who remember Samantha Smith.

Star: Later we went to Brooklyn, to Public School #276. When we got to the school, Katya and I were presented with flowers. Then we went into a room where we got to rest and have cookies with Mr. Grossberg, the school principal. After that, we had an assembly with hundreds of children, and I got to do my ballet, "A Prayer for Peace."

The school kids sang for us—both the national anthem of the Soviet Union and the American national anthem. After the long assembly was over, we ate lunch—chicken, greens, sweet potatoes and ICE CREAM! It was good! Then we saw some of the classrooms, and Katya and I were given pretty stickers and T-shirts. Katya gave the kids doves cut out of paper. One side had the address of a Soviet child, and the other was to be filled in by a U.S. child. That way, they can become pen pals.

The whole group was treated to a few moments of rest and some refreshments in the principal's office of Public School #276 in Brooklyn. The girls had student escorts for the three hours they were there, and all the teachers came to say hello, too. At a huge assembly that was led by the student body officers, Katya answered questions about Russia.

Katya: I enjoyed the concert at the school in Brooklyn very much. The kids had tried very hard to learn the Russian song "Polyushko-Polye" especially for us, their Soviet guests. Star performed her peace dance, and I played the piano and sang, "May There Always Be Sunshine." I hoped that the kids would join in because I knew that Samantha had loved that song and that many children in America could sing it in English. But the kids at the school did not know the words, so Mummy and I sang it. I decided that I would teach Star to sing it with me, and then she would share the words and the music with all her friends. Star liked the song.

After the concert the children took Star and me on a tour of the school. In each classroom the kids talked to us, showed us what they liked to do, and gave us things. They said they had been very busy preparing for my visit and had even made a kind of wall sheet with pictures about the USSR. When I began to tell them about Moscow, the Pioneers' Palace, and all my friends, there was no end to their questions. I saw that the children wanted to hear as much as they could about my country, because they hadn't really known anything about it before.

Star: When we left the school in Brooklyn, we went to the United Nations and posed in front of all the flags of the world.

Katya: The Soviet flag was there. I spotted it at once. Star and I were given special cards, which had only been given to grown-ups before. We were told that it was the first time children had been received like that at the United Nations. We went up in the elevator and met an under-secretary of the United Nations, Mr. Dayal. He said that Secretary-General Perez de Cuellar was very sorry that he had had to go away on business. He said the secretary-general had specially asked him to give Star and me his greetings.

Star: We were given a tour of the building and were presented with UN medals.

Katya: Then we were taken to the meeting room of the United Nations Security Council, and I was allowed to sit in the chair of the Soviet representative.

We were also shown the Economic and Social Council room and the General Assembly Hall. After the tour some press people asked me what I would say if I had a chance to speak at the UN. I said,

The girls took turns playing a computer game.

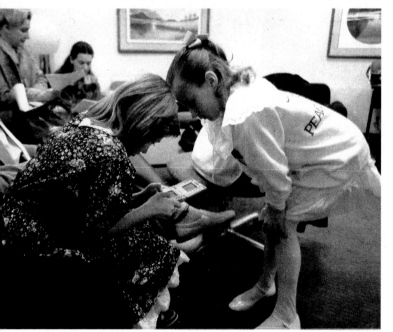

Everyone was excited by the prospect of touring the United Nations building. Marina took notes of everything that happened for her Good Times Book.

"Can I?", but they laughed and said it was only a joke. I sighed, because I would very much like to speak to all the nations and tell them that not only this year, but every year from now on, should be a year of peace. This means, of course, that the arms race must stop, and all the money that is now spent on weapons must be used to buy books, medicines, and toys for kids. Then no child on this planet would be hungry, illiterate, or unhappy. We must do it.

Before leaving, Star and I went to see the gifts that different countries have given to the UN. The one I liked best was the Soviet sputnik model. It caught the sun where it stood right next to the window, and the sun made it shine like a lovely ball of gold. There were two other beautiful gifts that I liked a lot: a huge carpet, made by American women, with the national insignia of all the UN member countries; and an ivory city carved by Chinese craftsmen.

Star shook hands with the U.S. Ambassador to the United Nations Vernon Walters while Soviet Ambassador Yuri Dubinin smiled. They had the girls sign a special registry.

Star: We then went to the Hyatt Hotel for a little rest. That night we went to dinner with Mr. and Mrs. James Roberts and their three children, and I spilled apple juice on Katya. It was another funny experience. I was a little embarrassed, because I was on my way to becoming the spill queen of the trip. Katya went to the theater to see *Big River*, but I stayed in the hotel because I was getting a cold, too.

Katya: In the evening I went to see *Big River*, a musical about the adventures of Huck Finn. All the characters spoke with a Southern accent that I had trouble understanding, but I knew what they were saying and singing. I don't think I have ever heard such beautiful voices. I wish that I could have taped them.

During the intermission people with kids and even some without kids came up to Mummy and me. They all said they were glad that a Soviet girl had come to America on a mission of peace, and they very much wanted me to like their country and wanted us all to become great friends.

After the performance all the actors gathered on the stage and I was invited to join them. They gave me a *Big River* T-shirt. And Mark Twain himself was standing right next to me! Well, at least he looked very much like Mark Twain himself, and I thought that the whole thing was very nice. I gave them some pictures of the shows of the Young Muscovites' Theatre that we have at the Pioneers' Palace back home. The actors were quite surprised and, I think, pleased to get these pictures as a gift from their young colleagues in the Soviet Union.

That night Mummy turned on the TV in our hotel, and we watched *Rocky IV*. I felt terrible. Soviet people don't look and act like that. There was not a word in that film that was true.

Katya felt at home with the cast of "Big River." She posed with them after the show. "I had a little bit of trouble understanding the Southern accents," she told Mark Twain.

Washington

Katya: We flew to Washington next.

Star: When we got off the plane, there were signs that read, "Welcome to Washington, D.C., Katya and Star." And once again children presented us with flowers. There were also more police and barriers. Pat said it was like traveling with a rock group.

Katya: One gray-haired man was holding a poster above his head that said, "Welcome, Katerina," and there was an inscription on his cap that said "Veterans for Peace." My friends explained to me that it was an organization of Americans who fought together with the Soviet army towards the end of World War II. Our countries were friends then.

This "Welcome to the U.S.A." cake was typical of the gestures of love offered by Americans to Katya. The whole group ate the cake and celebrated being together and becoming friends.
   In Washington, D.C., the girls attended a press conference that included reporters from the Children's Express. The press conference followed a big assembly at Wheatley Elementary School.

Both girls felt anxiety as well as excitement as they
waited for their meeting with President Reagan.

Next we went to a school and were welcomed by the kids and their president. That's what they call the head of the student council. The president was eleven years old and no taller than me. At first he tried to look very important, but then we began talking and playing and making jokes together.

Katya with her Peace Doves.

Star: When we got to the school, we went to an assembly where we were presented with beautiful gifts such as shirts and knitted sweaters and scrapbooks. Then we went upstairs and had cookies. Katya had hot cocoa and I accidently spilled it on her. I gave Katya my tights, since hers were now wet with cocoa. A woman from the PTA washed and ironed Katya's dress. The police had ordered an ambulance, because they thought she was burned. I felt awful, but I was glad

Katya wasn't really burned. All this made us very late for everything. After that scene, we had a peace talk, and Katya gave out her doves of peace again.

Katya: The cocoa spill really wasn't so bad. Star looked so miserable that Mummy patted her and tried to comfort her. I, too, wanted to say something nice to her, so I said, "I know what it is, Star. Every person has the right to a hobby. Dogs are my hobby, and spilling stuff on people is yours. So what's the big deal?" Star looked at me gratefully and we hugged. The bad moment was over.

The kids at the school had prepared quite a program for us. They handed us the lyrics of American peace songs so we could sing along with the choir. Then a few kids began dancing to some Russian music. They tried very hard, but it was clear that they did not really know the steps of a Russian dance. Their costumes weren't like ours at home, but they were very pretty. Then I jumped down from the platform and started whirling, showing them all the dance figures that I knew. The kids stopped at once and began clapping their hands, and then joined me in dancing.

Star: At a big press conference, there were reporters from the Children's Express—kids were interviewing us, too!

The girls became adept at keeping their composure when microphones and TV cameras were thrust at them.

45

These children guided Katya and Star around Wheatley School. Everyone was full of questions for Katya about life in the Soviet Union.

Mayor Barry of Washington, D.C. presented Katya with a scroll, making it "Katya Lycheva Day" in his city. A man there sang a song he had written for Samantha Smith. It made everyone cry, it was so beautiful.

Katya: After the concert the kids conducted their own press conference. I answered their questions about my friends, my school, and the Young Pioneers.

One boy asked me if people in the Soviet Union knew about the *Challenger* disaster. I said that everybody knew about that great tragedy. It had been caused by a machine that went wrong. "And what if someday there are weapons in space," I said. "Then the lives of people everywhere will depend on some machines that could break down. Space must be peaceful!"

A woman reporter asked what, in my opinion, the difference was between Soviet and American children. I said that I thought kids are the same the world over. They all like sweets, girls play with dolls, and boys like toy cars. Our interests and our dreams are very much alike: children everywhere want to be friends and to live in peace. I also said that we look alike. Then I couldn't help laughing because I remembered how one of the teachers had become confused when we came into her classroom. She pointed to me and said, "Children, this is Star Rowe," and then embraced Star and said, "and this is Katya Lycheva, our little visitor from the Soviet Union." Star and I looked at each other for a moment, but then we decided to admit who was who.

From the school we went on to see Marion Barry, the mayor of Washington, D.C. After that we were taken to a Ringling Brothers circus show.

Star: That night was the most exciting part of the day in Washington. Katya and I were promised a chance to ride some of the circus animals. We also got to feed and pet the unicorn. The animals we got to ride were an elephant and a horse. When we got on the elephant, I held on and the elephant rose up, and Katya and I screamed and our eyes bulged out. It was quite an experience for both of us. Then we rode the horse and that was exciting, too. I loved the circus. Later I saw a circus in Russia, and it was really good, too.

At the Ringling Brothers circus the two girls rode an elephant. When it reared up, Star got quite a thrill. Katya's trip was big news everywhere—even at the circus her picture was being taken. But the press people were nice and seemed to have a good time.

A colorful chariot of Pegasus, the winged horse, paraded Katya and Star and children from the Wheatley Elementary School around the circus ring. The crowd waved at Katya and she laughed with joy and loved it all.

Katya: Before we left the circus, Patricia Montandon told us that President Reagan would see Star and me at the White House at nine o'clock the next morning. That night I couldn't get to sleep for a long time. I kept thinking about the important meeting tomorrow.

In the morning I looked again at the gift I'd brought for the President: a blue globe with a broad smile, greeting all people with one hand and holding a white dove with the other.

Before we left the hotel, Star showed me a Children as the Peacemakers button and said she was going to give it to Mr. Reagan. I thought it would be a good thing to give the President something from the Soviet peace movement, too, so I put a Soviet Peace Committee scarf on my blue globe. Now the globe looked even happier.

Star: At 8:00 A.M. the next day we went on a tour of the White House. We had a 9:00 appointment to meet President Reagan. He was tall and smiled at us. That was a very big moment for both Katya and me. Before we gave President Reagan our presents, a man took our presents and put them through an X-ray machine. He said this was to make sure they were safe for the President to receive. The present from Katya was a felt globe that was waving one hand and holding a dove of peace in the other hand. This globe of peace had been made by schoolchildren from the Soviet Union. I gave President Reagan a pin that read "Children as the Peacemakers." He thanked me and said he would do what he could for peace. He also said that he thought it was very good for this

trip to take place, and he was glad I was hosting Katya on this trip. He then hugged me and Katya.

Katya: I gave the globe to the President and said that it had been made by kids to show that all Soviet children and all our people want peace. Children cannot live happily on Earth, I said, while there are nuclear weapons. I know that my country has made a proposal to eliminate all nuclear weapons on our planet before I grow up. That would be great! Then all children everywhere would be happy.

Mr. Reagan replied that he is no longer a child but he too would be happy to have peace, and he promised to do his best to free the Earth of nuclear weapons. I hope so. All kids want peace, and we're scared of a nuclear war.

Star: Katya and I also got to meet Mrs. Reagan's dog. His name is Rex. He was rambunctious like any normal puppy is. He was also very cute. When we left, we went to the Lincoln Memorial, with lots of press people following us. They were unhappy that they weren't let in for our appointment with President Reagan.

Later we went to the Soviet Embassy to visit a man from the Soviet Union. The embassy was beautiful, with lots of mirrors and curved windows and crystal chandeliers. The sofas and chairs were covered with brocade. I've never seen anything that pretty.

Katya presented President Ronald Reagan with a smiling globe of the world; it held a dove in one hand. Katya spoke in Russian, with Dimitri translating. Katya told the President, "Children cannot live happily on Earth while there are nuclear weapons."

Katya was able to visit the school for the children of the Russian Embassy officials and staff during her time in Washington, D.C.

The man, Acting Ambassador Oleg Sokolov, gave Katya a book on Washington. He gave me a doll from the Soviet Union that you are supposed to put over a teapot to keep it warm. I really liked the doll. I named it Katya. The ambassador also gave us flowers.

When we left the embassy, we went to a going-away party. We ate burgers and fries. After that we went to a museum. Then Katya and I went to another room where we were given presents. When we went to our hotel, we were given a huge cake that said in red, white, and blue, "Welcome to the U.S.A., Katya," and we got whatever soft drinks we wanted. Katya and I played at being waiters. We had a lot of fun that night with the adults, laughing and talking, even though there were lots of men and women around who were security people. We all relaxed and felt safe.

The security guards stayed in the hall outside our rooms all night. We also had the entire hotel floor just for us. I noticed that we now used service elevators and back doors whenever we could, because there was always a big crowd of people waiting for Katya. She wanted to talk to everyone, but the security people wouldn't let her.

"This is the most beautiful room I've ever seen," said Star when she was ushered into the Soviet Embassy's reception salon. Katya and Star entertained everyone by singing together as Katya played the accompaniment on the piano.

Star felt a little nervous dancing in such a beautiful place . . . but, as always, she was willing to try, even without her toe shoes. Katya played the piano as Star danced.

Houston

Katya: Houston, Texas, was the fourth city I visited in the United States.

Star: When we first got there, we were greeted by one hundred girl scouts in green uniforms. They gave us each a yellow rose of Texas, and Katya was given girl scout cookies. I was, too.

Then we got on a Texas covered wagon and rode to a store where we were each given cowgirl clothes, including boots and even a cowgirl hat. The adults were given blue jeans. Alevtina Fedulova from the Soviet Peace Committee and Marina, Katya's mom, laughed a lot. We were also each given a stuffed puppy. We thanked the manager and everyone else for all that they had done for us. We rode back to our hotel in the wagon. When we got there, we got to ride the horses of the Texas Rangers.

``Howdy, Katya. Welcome to Texas,'' the sign said at the airport as one hundred girl scouts greeted her in Houston. They had yellow roses for her and called her the yellow rose of Texas.

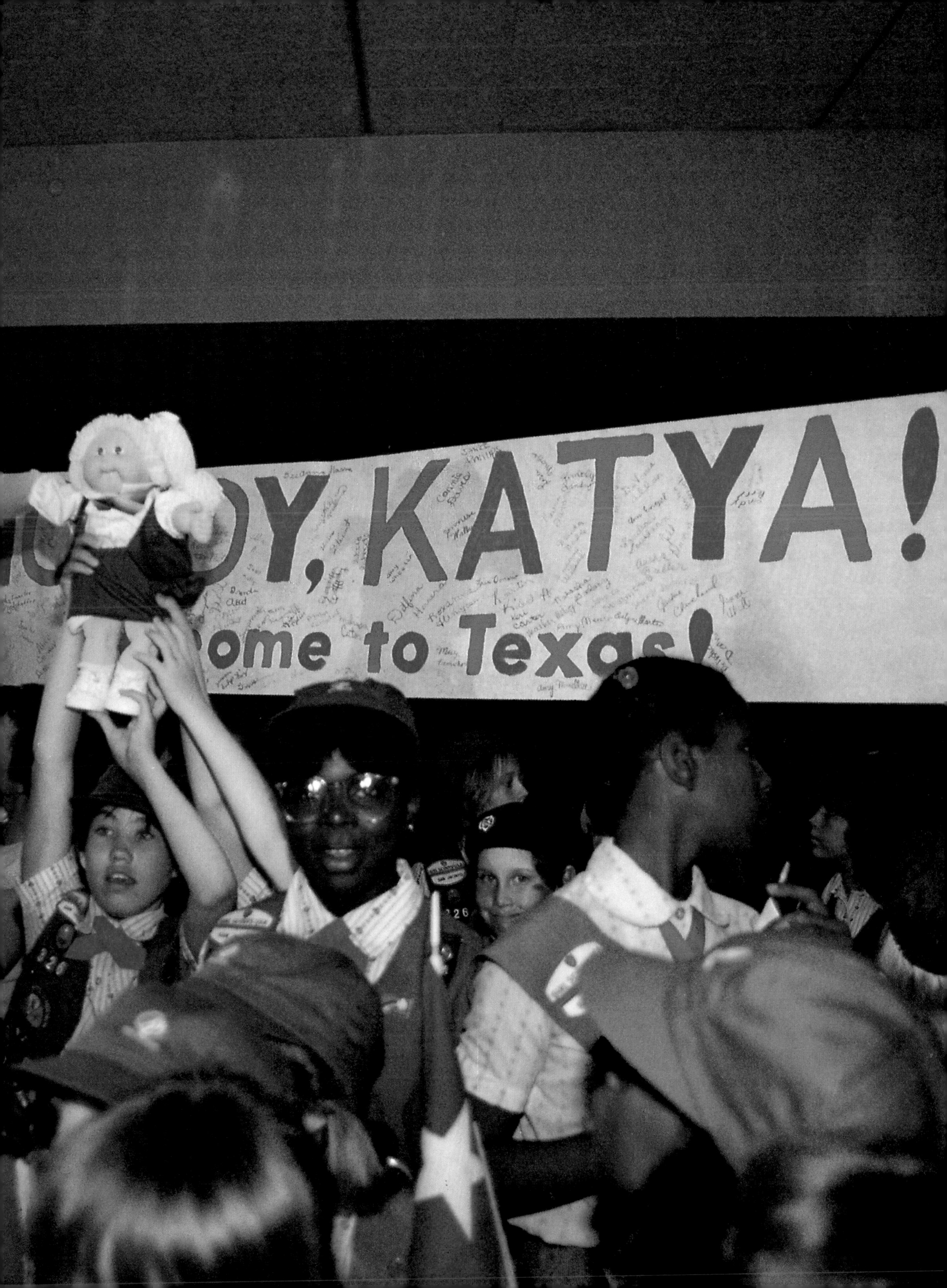
KATYA!
to Texas!

The girls were quickly outfitted in cowgirl clothes and taken for a ride in a covered wagon. Texas hospitality was evident—many people wanted to entertain Katya even though it was the Easter holiday.

A hand-painted sign said, "To Katya the Peace Child." Everyone was touched by the message.

On the Gulf of Mexico the girl scouts have a big house called Casa Mara. They greeted "Katerina" with a sign and sang a song.

WELC

KATRINA

"May I ride your horse?" Katya asked the Texas Rangers. "Sure," came the reply, and off rode Katya.
(above) The girl scouts introduced Katya to games such as "London Bridge Is Falling Down." Katya was "it."

Katya: We had a lot of fun at Casa Mara, the girl scout camp. We ran around on the grass and on the beach of the Gulf of Mexico. I was dying for a swim, but the water was too cold. The kids taught me a lot of American games. Some of the games were just like ours, only with different names. I loved the dinner, especially the traditional Mexican food called tacos. And I went on my first-ever Easter egg hunt.

In the evening we had a bonfire. We sang and danced and played more games by the light of the fire and the moon. It was really great.

Star: The next day we went to NASA, where we posed in astronaut suits and saw mission control. It wasn't curved the way I thought it would be from watching TV. Then we got to go to Pat's sister Glendora Hill's house because there were too many people in the NASA cafeteria and "security" wouldn't let us eat there. Glendora sent out for pizza.

On her first-ever Easter Egg hunt, Katya presented an intent lone figure as she hunted for eggs at the girl scout house in El Lago, Texas. (above) With her new American friends Amy and Diana, Katya took a break. She learned the rules of hunting Easter eggs very quickly and soon had a full basket.

Katya: I had been to the space exhibit at the National Economic Exhibition in Moscow many times; now I had a chance to see the American satellites and spaceships. Mike Cahill, a man who works at NASA, showed us many fascinating things, including the lunar module in which American astronauts had landed on the moon. He also took us to a stand devoted to the Soviet–U.S. space program. There were pictures of the Soyuz-Apollo mission. I had seen the same pictures at the Moscow exhibit.

Marina and her daughter shared a moment together at an early evening campfire at Casa Mara (far left). Other scouts and their moms made a full square. Later everyone held hands and sang "Cumbaya."

As an escape from the scheduled activities, Katya and her mom were driven to a Houston shopping center to ice skate. The stores were closed, so Katya and Marina had the rink almost to themselves. It was a rare moment just for them.

Mission Control and Houston's NASA captivated Star. "I followed the *Challenger* space shot," said Star, "and saw lots of TV pictures of Mission Control. I thought it was curved." Katya had also followed the *Challenger* launch and knew all about the disaster. "Everyone in the Soviet Union felt very badly about it," Katya said.

Star: Katya and I and two girl scouts, Kaela and Amy, got to play hide-and-go-seek tag at Glendora's. When Katya was "it," I hid in the back of a pick-up truck. I saw Katya coming and I jumped off the truck and hurt my foot. Pat called for an emergency check-up because Dimitri the interpreter told her that I should get my foot X-rayed. It turned out that I had pulled a ligament and had to be on crutches for a week. Katya took care of me, though, and it didn't hurt much.

When we got back from the hospital, we had to get right onto the bus to go to Casa Mara. When we got there, we went on an Easter egg hunt, and someone helped me since I was on crutches. I found nine eggs. I found the big egg, too. After egg hunting we went down to the beach. Then we drew pictures for peace.

We had tacos for dinner, with tomatoes and meat, and for dessert we had a chocolate sundae—delicious!! Then we went back down to the beach because we were going to have a campfire. When the campfire began, an Indian wearing a red and white feathered headdress came. He told us to concentrate on the fire being lit. What he did almost worked because we saw smoke come from the wood, but eventually we had to use matches. When the fire was finally started, we sang songs. One of them was "Cumbaya"—I think that means "by and by."

Then it was time to go home, but before we left for the hotel we were presented with gifts. Katya and I were given a key to the city. After we were given all the gifts, we went back to our hotel and went right to sleep.

Katya in space? Not really, but it certainly looks like it. At the Lyndon B. Johnson Space Center she posed behind this suit made of plywood. Her smile tells the story, and (below) a very tired girl fell asleep at last.

Los Angeles

Star: It was nighttime when we got to Los Angeles, but there were a lot of press people at the airport. I couldn't understand why. Pat explained that it was because Katya was the first Soviet girl to come on a peace mission to the United States.

Katya: The next morning a big group of children wearing different national costumes gathered in the hotel's biggest room. I had a Russian "Matrioshka" costume in my room, so I slipped away and quickly put it on. The choir sang "It's a Small World" in six different languages, and I performed a Russian dance called "Barynia." I think my costume was a success.

This touring display sponsored by the United Nations honors Samantha Smith, the young American who traveled to the Soviet Union for the cause of world peace. Katya and Star spoke of Samantha often during their travels. (right) Katya and Star received a large plaque from representatives of the city of Los Angeles.

After my dance, Patricia Montandon said she had a surprise for me. She asked me to close my eyes. When I opened my eyes again after a few minutes, you could have knocked me over with a feather. Patricia was holding a cocker spaniel puppy in her hands. It was her present to me. I was so happy. Mummy and I decided to call the puppy Bim.

The International Children's Choir sang at the breakfast hosted by the Hyatt Hotel in Los Angeles. Their voices blended beautifully as they sang "Let There Be Peace on Earth" and "It's a Small World."
  Wearing a Russian "Matrioshka" costume, Katya did an impromptu dance. Everyone applauded at her show of fun and spirit.

"All Katya thinks about is peace and dogs," Marina had said one day. Katya was so delighted when Patricia presented her with a cocker spaniel that she hugged her and then the puppy (whom Katya later named Bim) over and over again. Star and Patricia later went to Moscow to deliver Bim, because he had to have the proper papers to get into the Soviet Union and they couldn't be prepared while Katya was in the United States.

Star: Later we went to the Commonwealth Elementary School, where they had an outdoor assembly. It was warm and sunny. Someone gave Katya sunglasses, and she looked just like a movie star when she put them on. We exchanged gifts, and then we had a peace talk with the children. The kids were very interested in peace and were surprised that Katya looked the same as an American child. They thought she would look different because she is Russian.

At the Commonwealth Avenue public school in Los Angeles, the students held an outdoor assembly. Katya and Patricia displayed the Children as the Peacemakers flag as Patricia told the children how Children as the Peacemakers belongs to them and all the other children of the world. Katya handed out her peace doves.

When we left the school, we went to Universal Studios. We met actors dressed as the Son of Frankenstein and Woody Woodpecker and Charlie Chaplin. We went to visit King Kong. Then we went on a tour of Universal Studios. All kinds of things happened. For example, the shark called "Jaws" came roaring toward us. Katya and I were scared to death. We looked at each other and hugged.

Later we met with the Los Angeles City Council. They even had a long red carpet for us out on the sidewalk.

"Jaws nearly got us!" said Star. At Universal Studios it all seemed so real that everyone hung on for dear life. The two girls were caught in the clutches of a monstrous King Kong at Universal. Katya inspected his gross teeth and didn't seem at all afraid.

Surrounded at Universal Studios by actors dressed as Charlie Chaplin, Woody Woodpecker, Frankenstein's monster, and Conan the Barbarian, Katya played nurse to Star, who had pulled a ligament in her foot.

Katya: The Los Angeles City Council was in session, but the grown-ups interrupted it and gave the floor to me—"a little Soviet girl who has come to our country on a mission of peace."

I said I would never forget the warm welcome I had received in America from children and adults alike, and I would tell everybody back home about all my new friends and certainly about my best friend, Star Rowe. "Before I leave," I said to the members of the council, "I want to tell all children and adults in the United States that Soviet people cherish peace. They work for it and want to be friends with all nations. Let's try to work together."

This was Katya's view of the Los Angeles City Council. This drawing was a gift from Katya to the city of Los Angeles. She presented it at a session of the Los Angeles City Council. (next page) The council had set aside a special time to greet Katya and tell her how happy Americans were about her trip.

Star: Katya and I were presented with gifts and then we left. Everyone we meet wants peace—I can't understand why we can't have it. I know if we keep working for it, we *can have* it.

We had a special dinner that night with the Nelson family of Glendale. They even had a swimming pool, but Katya's mom wouldn't let Katya swim. She was afraid Katya would get sick again.

Katya learned how similar people are throughout the world as she visited with her American host families. (right) Minnie and Mickey Mouse welcome the peace children to Disneyland.

After that came the best part of the whole trip—DISNEYLAND! When we first got there, we met Mickey and Minnie Mouse. We signed a guest book. Then we rode some kind of cable car, but only to get to one of the rides. That was the jungle cruise. We saw all kinds of tribes, and we saw elephants and a waterfall. We got to see many different animals, but of course they were not real although they sure looked real. After lunch we went to "Sing America." It had hundreds of puppets that sang to music. It was fun, but then we went on a big ride—one that can really shake you up, if you know what I mean—the Space Mountain. That was the most fun. But Alevtina looked very pale when she got off. Katya looked pale, too, and I must have also, since my knees felt wobbly.

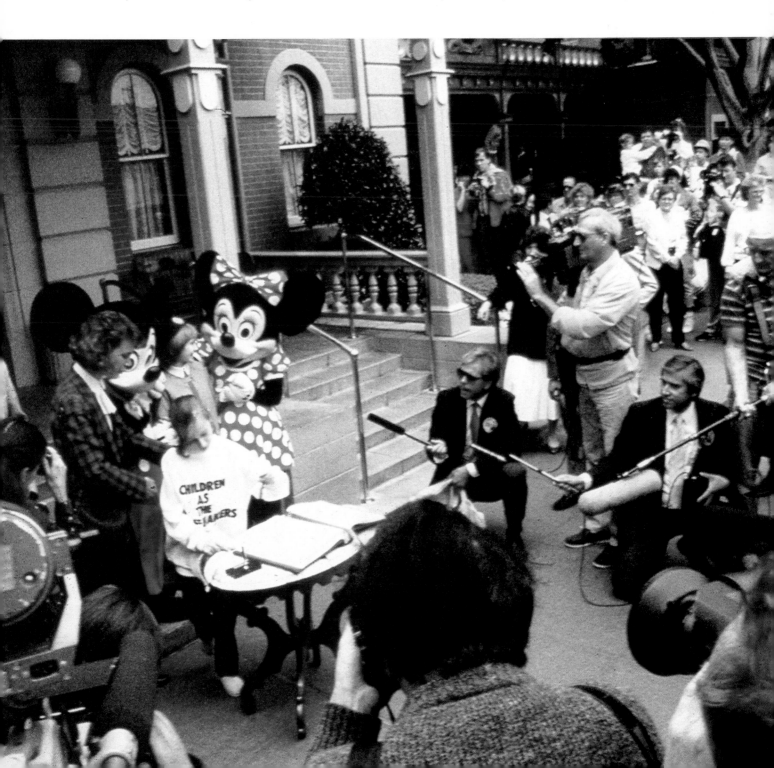

Katya and Star left the press behind as they set off on a cruise along Disneyland's jungle rivers.

Katya: It's a fairyland. We saw a show in which puppets sang and danced, and we went on a jungle cruise and looked at the wild animals and their little ones. Many of the puppets were cartoon characters that I recognized. Disneyland is special. I love it there.

Star: When it was time for Katya to go back to Moscow, I felt sad because we had become such good friends. We both want to grow up in a peaceful world and not have nuclear war. I want to be a ballerina. I have studied ballet since I was two years old. Katya wants to be a movie director. I think all of the children we met are afraid of war. I know I am. I know Katya is, too. So are my friends.

I had to say goodbye to Katya at the hotel freight elevator at 3:00 A.M. I hugged her and cried.

Katya: The time had come to say goodbye. I was already missing my family and friends and feeling not a little homesick. All the same, I hated to leave my new friends. I told them I would miss them when I was back in Moscow. They said, "Don't forget us, Katya. Come again." And I thought how great it would be if they could come to the Soviet Union— we would make them very welcome.

I nearly cried when I said goodbye to Star. I love her very much. We both know there is no reason why Soviet and American kids can't be friends. Maybe the grown-ups have all those problems because they had no chance to become friends when they were kids. Well, then, we must try very hard to grow up and still be friends.

Star and I parted with a dream of peace, because if we don't have it, none of us will live—kids or grown-ups.

Katya Lycheva, the Soviet ambassador of peace, symbolically held a fragile world in her hands . . . a world all children have in common.

The President of the U.S.S.R., Andrei Gromyko, met with Katya and Star during a Children As the Peacemakers trip to Moscow. "I like very much your work for peace," he said.